Meeks Heit
Publishing Company

Violence Prevention

special me
and
violence-
free

Linda Meeks · Philip Heit · Randy Page

Edited by Julie DeVillers

Everyday Learning Corporation
Editorial, Sales, and Customer Service Office
P.O. Box 812960
Chicago, IL 60681

Director of Editorial: Julie DeVillers
Director of Art and Design: Jim Brower
Graphic Designer: Deborah Rubenstein
Editorial Assistant: Jill Keyerleber
Director of Marketing: David Willcox

Printed in the United States of America.

4 5 6 7 8 9 EB 04 03

ISBN 0-9630009-9-3

Table of Contents

Chapter 1

You Are Special

You are special.

How can you tell you are special?

No one is just like you.

No one looks just like you.

No one acts just like you.

That makes you special.

This is a book for a special person.

This special person is you.

This book tells you how to take care of you.

You know how to take care of your toys.

You know how to take care of your books.

You are more important than your books or toys.

You need to know how to take care of you.

Say this Special Me
and Violence-Free Pledge.

No matter where I go,

No matter what I see,

I know that I am special,

So I will take good care of me.

Chapter 2

Violence Is Wrong

You need to stay safe.

You need to protect yourself.

You need to watch out for violence.

Do you know about violence?

Do you know what violence is?

Violence is anything that hurts someone
or something.

If someone tries to hurt you, that is violence.

If someone tries to break your toy, that is violence.

Violence harms people.

Hitting a person is violence.

Calling a person a mean name is violence.

Shooting a person with a gun is violence.

Grown-ups are harmed by violence.

Children are harmed by violence, too.

Violence harms things.

Breaking a window is violence.

Taking candy from a store is violence.

Writing on a building is violence.

Violence is wrong!

It is wrong to harm another person.

It is wrong to harm things.

Violence is wrong.

You need to know that violence is wrong.

Say this Special Me and Violence-Free Pledge.

No matter where I go,

No matter what I see,

I will not be violent,

To take good care of me.

Chapter 3

Victims Of Violence

A **victim** is someone who is harmed by violence.

Violence always has a victim.

Never harm another person.

A victim might be harmed in many ways.

A victim might have a cut or a broken bone.

A victim's bike might be stolen.

A victim might become afraid.

A victim might not be able to sleep at night.

A victim might feel sad.

A victim might feel angry.

A victim might not feel safe.

Can you think of a time when you did not feel safe?

Did you feel afraid?

Did you feel alone?

What should you do if you have been a victim?

Get help from a grown-up you trust.

Tell the grown-up what happened.

Do not keep secrets.

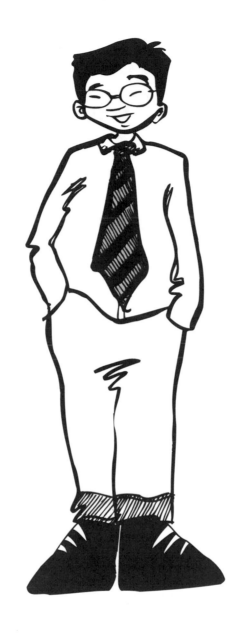

When you do not feel safe, tell a grown-up you trust.

This grown-up can help you feel better.

This grown-up can help you stay safe.

Say this Special Me and Violence-Free Pledge.

When I do not feel safe,

I will tell a grown-up I trust.

I will not be a victim,

Staying safe is a must.

Chapter 4

People Who Help You Stay Safe

Other grown-ups help you stay safe.

A safety guard helps you cross the street.

A police officer looks out for people who might harm you.

Your mother may tell you to stay in your yard.

Your teacher may tell you to cross the street at the crosswalk.

Your father may tell you to stay close when you are at the mall.

These grown-ups tell you to follow rules.

It is important for you to follow rules.
Rules are made to help you stay safe.
People who do not follow rules may be
harmed by violence.

Say this Special Me and Violence-Free Pledge.

Many grown-ups help me stay safe,

At home and play and school.

When grown-ups give me rules to follow,

I will follow every rule.

Chapter 5

Making Wise Choices

You make choices every day.

You may choose what to wear.

You may choose what to play.

It is important to make wise choices.

What is a wise choice?

A wise choice is a healthful choice.

A wise choice follows laws and school rules.

A wise choice follows family rules.

A wise choice shows you care about others.

A wise choice helps keep you safe.

Suppose someone asks you to harm another person.

A person might want you to break a window.

A person might want you to do something unsafe.

Say NO!

How do you say NO?

Look at the person.

Say NO.

Tell the person why you are saying NO.

Act like you mean what you say.

Do not change your mind.

If someone wants you to push another person,
say NO.

Look at the person.

Say, "Pushing a person is violent.

I will not be violent."

If someone tells you to call someone a mean name,
say NO.

Look at the person.

Say, "Calling someone a mean name is wrong.

I will not be violent."

Say this Special Me and Violence-Free Pledge.

I make many choices,

About what I do and what I say.

I will be sure to make wise choices,

To protect me every day.

Chapter 6

Feeling Angry

Do you ever get angry?

Of course you do!

Some people think getting angry is bad.

That is not true.

Everyone gets angry sometimes.

Anger is a feeling.

You can show your feelings.

Your face can show your feelings.

Your body can show your feelings.

Do you know what happens to your body
when you get angry?
You breathe faster.
Your heart beats faster.
Your face might turn red.

Sometimes people who are angry become violent.

They may start a fight.

They may try to harm someone.

Suppose you are angry.

Do not act in violent ways.

Talk to a grown-up about your angry feelings.

Ask a grown-up what to do.

Run around your yard until you feel calm.

Draw a picture about what made you angry.

Share your picture with a grown-up.

Say this Special Me and Violence-Free Pledge.

When I feel angry,

I know fighting need not be.

I will talk to a grown-up I trust,

To take good care of me.

Respecting Others

Showing respect for others helps keep you safe.

There are many ways that you can show respect.

Using manners shows respect.

Say "please" and "thank you."

Say "I am sorry" when you make a mistake.

Listen to others when they talk.

Be kind to others.

Never call a person a mean name.

Never cut in line.

Maybe you have met a bully.

A **bully** is a person who wants to hurt or scare someone.

A bully might try to take your lunch money.

A bully might call you a mean name.

A bully does not show respect for others.

A bully is violent.

People who do not show respect for others
may be violent.

They may call you a mean name.

They may try to steal something that belongs
to you.

They may try to hurt you.

People who do not show respect for others
may become victims.

They may make other people angry with
their actions.

Other people may try to harm them.

Say this Special Me and Violence-Free Pledge.

I will show respect for other people,

So they will show respect for me.

I will be kind and use good manners,

To help take good care of me.

Stay Away From Fights

Sometimes people disagree.

Two people may want to use the swing at the same time.

Two people may want to play with the same toy.

When two people disagree, they may get angry.

They may feel like fighting.

Fighting is a kind of violence.

45

Suppose you disagree with someone.
What can you do?

Show respect for the other person.
Share your feelings with the other person.
Let the other person share feelings with you.
Listen to the other person.
If you have made a mistake, say, "I am sorry."

Suppose someone wants you to fight.

You might get hurt if you fight.

Run away.

Talk to a grown-up.

Tell a grown-up about the disagreement.

Say This Special Me and Violence-Free Pledge

I show respect to people,

Even when we disagree.

I do not fight with other people,

And that takes good care of me.

Chapter 9

Stay Away From Strangers

A stranger is someone you do not know.

A stranger may be a male.

A stranger may be a female.

A stranger may look like anyone else.

A stranger may act friendly.

Most strangers do not harm people.

But, some strangers do harm people.

Some strangers harm children.

It is important for you to follow rules around strangers.

Never talk to strangers.

A stranger may know your name.

A stranger may ask you where you live.

Never tell a stranger where you live.

A stranger may try to give you candy.

Never take candy from a stranger.

A stranger may ask you to ride in a car.
A stranger may say that something bad
happened to your parents.
The stranger may say your parents want
you to ride in the car.
Do not go near a stranger's car.
Never get into a car with a stranger.
Run away.

If a stranger bothers you in any way, run away.

Run away as fast as you can.

Yell as loud as you can.

Tell a grown-up about the stranger.

Say this Special Me and Violence-Free Pledge.

When a stranger wants to drive me,

A mighty NO is what I will say.

If a stranger tries to talk to me,

I will yell and run away.

Chapter 10

Ways To Keep Your Body Safe

Private means something that belongs only to you.

Your body is private.

Your body belongs to you.

You have a right to protect your body.

You have a right to make choices about
your body.

You can choose who will see your private
body parts.

Private body parts are body parts covered
by a bathing suit.

You can choose who will touch your private
body parts.

A **safe touch** is a touch that feels right.

A safe touch can be a touch from a trusted adult.

A parent holding your hand is a safe touch.

A doctor checking your body is a safe touch.

An **unsafe touch** is a touch that does not feel right.

An unsafe touch is a touch that you do not like.

Suppose someone tickles you and you do not like it.

This is an unsafe touch because you do not like it.

Suppose someone touches a private body part.

This person might be a stranger.

This person might be someone you know.

It might be a babysitter or a teacher.

It might be someone in your family.

You have the right to tell someone not to touch you.

Tell the person to stop.

Be firm.

Yell as loud as you can.

Run away from this person.

Always tell a grown-up you trust about
an unsafe touch.

Tell the grown-up about the person who
touched you.

Tell the grown-up where the person touched you.

If the grown-up does not believe you, tell
another grown-up.

Say this Special Me and Violence-Free Pledge.

I know my body is private,

It belongs to me in every way.

If someone touches me with an unsafe touch,

I will yell and run away.

Stay Away From Drugs

A **drug** is something that changes the way the body and mind work.

Some drugs can help the body.

Some drugs can harm the body.

Alcohol is a kind of drug.

Some drugs are pills.

Some drugs are smoked in a cigarette.

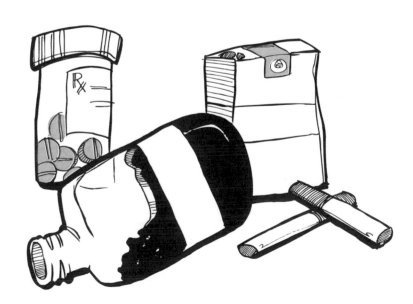

Drugs can change the way a person thinks and acts.

People who use drugs may become violent.

They may harm others.

They may harm people around them.

Suppose someone you know uses drugs.

This person may become violent.

This person might harm you.

Stay away from this person.

Tell a grown-up you trust about the person
who uses drugs.

You can choose not to drink alcohol.

You can choose not to use other drugs.

You can say NO if someone asks you to take drugs.

You can try to stay away from people who
 use drugs.

Suppose someone offers you a harmful drug.

Suppose someone wants you to drink alcohol.

Say NO.

Look at the person.

Say, "NO, I will not take drugs.

"Drugs will change the way I think and feel."

Act like you mean what you say.

Do not change your mind.

Tell a trusted grown-up what happened.

Say this Special Me and Violence-Free Pledge.

If someone offers me harmful drugs,

A mighty NO is what I'll say.

If I see someone using drugs,

I will stay far away.

Chapter 12

Stay Away From Weapons

A **weapon** is an object used for fighting.

A weapon can be a gun.

A weapon can be a knife.

Weapons may be used to harm people.

Suppose you see a weapon.

Never touch the weapon.

Never play with the weapon.

Stay away from the weapon.

Find a grown-up.

Tell the grown-up about the weapon.

If you see a person carrying a weapon, run away.
Tell a trusted grown-up about the person.

Suppose you hear a gunshot.

Never look out the window when you hear a gunshot.

Stay away from the windows.

Stay away from the door.

Go into the bathroom, or a room with no windows.

Hide behind a couch or a big chair.

Lie down on the floor.

Find a grown-up as soon as you can.

Say this Special Me and Violence-Free Pledge.

I will never touch a weapon,

A weapon is not for play.

If I ever see a weapon,

I will run away.

Say the Special Me and Violence-Free Pledge.

No matter where I go,

No matter what I see,

I know that I am special,

So I will take good care of me.

No matter where I go,

No matter what I see,

I will not be violent,

To take good care of me.

When I do not feel safe,

I will tell a grown-up I trust.

I will not be a victim,

Staying safe is a must.

Many grown-ups help me stay safe,
At home and play and school.
When grown-ups give me rules to follow,
I will follow every rule.

I make many choices,
About what I do and what I say.
I will be sure to make wise choices,
To protect me every day.

When I feel angry,
I know fighting need not be.
I will talk to a grown-up I trust,
To take good care of me.

I will show respect for other people,
So they will show respect for me.
I will be kind and use good manners,
To help take good care of me.

I show respect to people,
Even when we disagree.
I do not fight with other people,
And that takes good care of me.

When a stranger wants to drive me,
A mighty NO is what I will say.
If a stranger tries to talk to me,
I will yell and run away.

I know my body is private,
It belongs to me in every way.
If someone touches me with an
unsafe touch,
I will yell and run away.

If someone offers me harmful drugs,
A mighty NO is what I'll say.
If I see someone using drugs,
I will stay far away.

I will never touch a weapon,
A weapon is not for play.
If I ever see a weapon,
I will run away.

Glossary and Index

Bully, page 41

A **bully** is a person who wants to hurt or scare someone.

Drug, page 63

A **drug** is something that changes the way the body and mind work.

Private, page 55

Private means something that belongs only to you.

Private body parts, page 56

Private body parts are body parts covered by a bathing suit.

Safe touch, page 57

A **safe touch** is a touch that feels right.

Stranger, page 49

A **stranger** is someone you do not know.

Unsafe touch, page 58

An **unsafe touch** is a touch that does not feel right and that you do not like.

Victim, page 15

A **victim** is someone who is harmed by violence.

Violence, page 10

Violence is anything that hurts someone or something.

Weapon, page 69

A **weapon** is an object used for fighting.